Keto Baking Recipe Book

Healthy Assortment of Delicious Ketogenic Diet Baking Recipes!

Copyright ©

All rights reserved. No part of this book may be reproduced, stored in a retrieval system, or transmitted in any form or by any means, electronic, mechanical, photocopying, recording, scanning, or otherwise, without the prior written permission of the publisher.

Disclaimer

All the material contained in this book is provided for educational and informational purposes only. No responsibility can be taken for any results or outcomes resulting from the use of this material.

While every attempt has been made to provide information that is both accurate and effective, the author does not assume any responsibility for the accuracy or use/misuse of this information.

INTRODUCTION

Hello! Thank you for taking the time to read this collection of Ketogenic Diet Recipes!

I have been on the Ketogenic Diet since 2012 and it has made tremendous improvements in my life! Being a cook and a food lover, I had to find ways to adapt my everyday diet to include all my favorite foods without cheating myself and my diet. This lead me to experiment with a lot of foods and come up with the best Ketogenic Diet recipes I could! I hope you enjoy them as much as I did!

What is a Ketogenic Diet?

A Ketogenic Diet is a Low Carb and High Fat Diet. The purpose of undergoing a Ketogenic Diet is to allow the body to go through the process of Ketosis. This process eliminates glucose in the body so that energy needs to be taken from stored fats instead of glucose. Essentially, this diet will force your body into this metabolic state through the starvation of carbs, as carbs lead to glucose in the body.

This new metabolic state will have you burning ketones instead of glucose. By doing this, you are creating many advantages for yourself. These include:

-Health

-Weight Loss

-Physical/Mental Performance

-Control of Blood Sugat

-Cholesterol/Blood Pressure

-Epilepsy

-Insulin Resistence

-Skin Care

Careful considerations need to be taken in your diet in order to achieve success in reaching ketosis and allowing yourself to feel these benefits. Some foods need to be taken more and some foods needs to be removed. In short:

Eat : Meats, Leafy Greens, Veggies, High Fat Dairy, Nuts + Seeds, Avocodo + Berries, Sweeteners, Other fats

Don't Eat: Grains (wheat, rice cereal), Sugar, Fruit (apples, bananas, oranges), Tubers (potatoes, yams)

The average person (who is not on a Ketogenic Diet) is recommended to have anywhere from 25g-35g of net carbs per day. However, on a Ketogenic Diet, it is recommended that a person ingests 15g of net carbs (or less) per day to reach Ketosis.

What is a Net Carb? All of the carbs minus the Dietary Fibre! I have tracked the Net Carbs for most recipes in this book and have included them in order to assist you in tracking your Net Carb counts.

I hope you enjoy this Ketogenic Baking Cookbook!

TABLE OF CONTENTS

Chewy Chocolate Chip Cookie 7

Soft and Chewy Cookies 9

Pecan Snowball Cookie 11

Flourless Chocolate Chip Cookies 13

Shortbread Cookies 15

Coconut Chip Cookies 17

Butter Cookie Energy Bites 19

Oreos 20

Pumpkin Cream Cheese Cookies 22

Coconut Cookies 24

Chocolate Fudge Cookie 25

Coconut Cluster 27

Almond Zucchini Cookies 28

Chocolate Cloud Cookies 29

Chocolate Sea Salt Cookies 31

Cinnamon Butter Cookie 33

Snickerdoodle Crème Cookies 34

Cream Cheese Brownie 36

Cinnamon Roll Mug Cake 38

Cocoa Butter Blondie 40

Pound Cake 42

Lemon Coconut Cake 44

Brownie Cupcakes 46

Cinnamon Bundt Cake **48**

Carrot Cake **50**

Butter Cake **52**

Avocado Brownies **54**

Chocolate Tart **56**

Chewy Chocolate Chip Cookie

Ingredients:

1/3 cup coconut oil, room temperature

1/2 cup grass-fed butter, room temperature

2 eggs

1 teaspoon vanilla extract

3/4 cup golden monk fruit sweetener

1/2 teaspoon baking soda

1/4 teaspoon cream of tartar

1/2 teaspoon pink Himalayan salt

3 cups almond flour

3 oz. 100% cacao baking chocolate bar

Directions:

Line two baking sheets with parchment paper and preheat oven to 350 degrees.

In a medium-sized bowl, using a hand mixer, mix together coconut oil and butter. Once combined, add eggs and vanilla extract and continue to mix with hand mixer.

In the same bowl, add monk fruit sweetener, baking soda, cream of tartar, and salt. Mix using hand mixer until well-combined.

One cup at a time, add almond flour and mix together with hand mixer.

In a bowl, microwave chocolate pieces in 15 second increments until just barely soft. Transfer chocolate to plastic baggie and carefully break pieces apart using a rolling pin or the bottom of a hard object. Pour chocolate pieces into bowl of dough and fold in until combined.

Form dough into balls and lightly press down and place on prepared cookie sheets, allowing plenty of room in between cookies for dough to spread during baking process.

Bake cookies for 18-20 minutes, until edges are golden brown.

Remove from oven and allow to cool completely before serving. Enjoy!

Number of Servings: 20

Net Carbs Per Serving: 1.9g

Soft and Chewy Cookies

Ingredients:

3/4 cup almond meal

1/4 cup shredded coconut

1 tablespoon baking powder

1/2 teaspoon stevia

1 tablespoon coconut oil melted

1 teaspoon vanilla extract

2 large eggs

Directions:

Combine the almond meal, shredded coconut, stevia, and baking powder in a bowl.

Combine the wet ingredients in a separate bowl and then add them to the dry ingredients. Mix until combined.

Drop dough on a cookie sheet (preferably covered with a silicone baking mat) about 2" apart. Makes eight large cookies or twelve small cookies.

Bake at 375 degrees for 15 minutes.

Let the cookies cool completely on a wire rack before eating.

Number of Servings: 8

Net Carbs Per Serving: 3g

Pecan Snowball Cookie

Ingredients:

8 tablespoons butter

1 1/2 cup almond flour

1 cup pecans, chopped

1/2 cup sweetener

1 teaspoon vanilla extract

1/2 teaspoon vanilla liquid stevia

1/4 teaspoon salt

extra confectioners to roll balls in

Directions:

Preheat oven to 350 degrees F.

Place all ingredients into food processor and process until batter forms a ball. Pulse if needed. Taste batter, adjust sweetener if needed.

Line a baking sheet with silpat or parchment.

Use a cookie scoop and make 24 mounds.

Roll each mound in the palm of your hand.

Place in freezer for 20-30 minutes.

Place in oven for 15 minutes or until golden around edges.

Allow to cool slightly.

Once able to handle roll each in some confectioners sweetener.

Allow to cool completely before storing in an air tight container.

Number of Servings: 24

Net Carbs Per Serving: 1g

Flourless Chocolate Chip Cookies

Ingredients:

1 ½ cups powdered Swerve sugar substitute

6 tablespoons unsweetened cocoa powder

¼ teaspoon salt

½ cup very dark chocolate chips

½ cup chopped pecans

3-4 large egg whites

1 teaspoon vanilla extract

Directions:

Heat oven to 350 degrees.

Cover baking sheet in baking parchment and spray with cooking spray.

Mix dry ingredients (Swerve, cocoa, salt, chocolate chips, and pecans) together in a mixing bowl.

Add vanilla with three egg whites and stir to moisten batter. If it is as very thick or all the dry ingredients aren't moistened add one more egg white. (The batter should be very soft / sticky, but not soupy.)

*Place rounded teaspoons of dough onto cookie sheet, 2"-3" apart as cookies will spread and thin while baking.

Bake for 11-12 minutes.

Cookies will still be soft in the center when removed from the oven. Allow them to set-up on the pan for 5-8 minutes before removing to cooling rack.

Number of Servings: 24

Net Carbs Per Serving: 1.3g

Shortbread Cookies

Ingredients:

2 1/2 cups almond flour

6 tablespoons butter (softened; can use coconut oil for dairy-free, but flavor and texture will be different) *

1/2 cup erythritol (or other granular sweetener of choice)**

1 teaspoom vanilla extract

Directions:

Preheat the oven to 350 degrees F. Line a cookie sheet with parchment paper.

Use a hand mixer or stand mixer to beat together the butter and erythritol, until it's fluffy and light in color.

Beat in the vanilla extract. Beat in the almond flour, 1/2 cup at a time. (The dough will be dense and a little crumbly, but should stick when pressed together.)

Scoop rounded tablespoonfuls of the dough onto the prepared cookie sheet. Flatten each cookie to about 1/3" thick. (You can make them thicker or thinner to your liking. Keep in mind they will not spread or thin out during baking, so make them as thin as you want them when done.)

Bake for about 12 minutes, until the edges are golden. Allow to cool completely in the pan before handling (cookies will harden as they cool).

Number of Servings: 18

Net Carbs Per Serving: 0.1g

Coconut Chip Cookies

Ingredients:

1 cup almond flour

1/2 cup cacao nibs

1/2 cup unsweetened coconut flakes

1/3 cup erythritol

1/2 cup almond butter

1/4 cup butter, melted

2 large eggs

20 drops liquid Stevia

1/4 teaspoon salt

Glaze (Optional):

1/4 cup heavy whipping cream

1/8 teaspoon guar gum

10 drops Liquid Stevia

1/2 teaspoon vanilla extract (optional)

Directions:

Pre-heat oven to 350°F. Mix together the dry ingredients: cacao nibs, almond flour, coconut flakes (unsweetened), erythritol and salt.

Melt the butter in the microwave, then mix together all of the wet ingredients: butter, almond butter, eggs and liquid stevia. You can optionally add some vanilla extract during this step if you wish.

Slowly pour the dry ingredients into the wet and mix together thoroughly.

On a parchment paper lined baking sheet (or silpat), spoon out cookies evenly spaced. You should get about 16 cookies in total.

Flatten the cookie dough with your fingers (or the back of a spoon). Don't over press the cookies, they should be about 1/3 inch thick.

Bake cookies for 20-25 minutes or until the edges are golden brown. Remove from the oven and let cool on a cooling rack.

Optionally, create a glaze by combining the heavy cream, sweetener, and extract. Use a small mixer (or immersion blender) to mix this together. Add the guar gum little by little while blending to thicken.

Glaze the top of the cookies. The mixture should be relatively thick, but it's best to put in the refrigerator so that it solidifies more.

Serve and enjoy!

Number of Servings: 16

Net Carbs Per Serving: 2.2g

Butter Cookie Energy Bites

Ingredients:

1 cup almond flour

3 tablespoons melted butter

2 tablespoons Swerve sweetener

1 teaspoon vanilla extract

Pinch of salt

Directions:

Combine all ingredients in a small bowl

The mixture should be wet enough to stick together

Scoop out 1 tbsp of the mixture at a time a roll into a ball

The balls should be 1 1/4 inch in diameter

Refrigerate for 1 hour, if desired

Number of Servings: 8

Net Carbs Per Serving: 1.6g

Oreos

Ingredients:

Cookies:

2 1/4 cups almond or hazelnut flour

3 tablespoons coconut flour

4 tablespoons cocoa powder

1 teaspoons baking powder

1/2 teaspoon xanthan gum

1/4 teaspoon salt

1/2 cup butter, softened

1/2 cup Swerve Sweetener

1 egg

1 teaspoon vanilla extract

Cream Filling:

4 oz. cream cheese – softened

2 tablespoons butter

1/2 teaspoons vanilla extract

1/2 cup powdered Swerve (you can grind granulated Swerve in a spice grinder)

Directions:

Pre-heat oven to 350 degrees.

In a medium bowl mix together the dry ingredients.

In a separate bowl, cream together the Swerve and butter until light and fluffy, about 2 minutes.

Add egg and vanilla, mix until fully combined.

Add dry ingredients and mix until combined.

Roll out dough between two sheets of waxed paper to a rectangle about 1/8 of an inch thick. Using a circle cutter, cut out as many cookies as you can. Place them onto a parchment-lined cookie sheet. Re-roll out cookie dough until you run out!

Bake cookies for 12 minutes. Let cool completely before filling.

To make filling:

Using a food processor, cream together cream cheese, and butter.

Mix in vanilla extract.

Gradually mix in powdered Swerve.

Number of Servings: 30-40

Pumpkin Cream Cheese Cookies

Ingredients:

1/2 cup coconut flour

3 oz cream cheese softened

1/2 cup pumpkin puree

1/2 cup butter, unsalted softened

1/2 cup erythritol

1 teaspoon vanilla extract

1 1/2 teaspoons pumpkin spice

1/4 teaspoon salt

Directions:

Preheat the oven to 180C/350F degrees.

Line a baking tray with parchment paper.

In a bowl, whisk the butter and erythritol (or sugar substitute of choice).

Add the cream cheese, vanilla extra and pumpkin and whisk until smooth.

Add the coconut flour, pumpkin spices and salt and beat until combined. The mixture will be sticky.

Wet your hands and take a ball of the dough.

Place on the baking tray and repeat for the rest of the dough.

Gently press down on the dough balls, either with a spoon or your hands.

Use a fork to make a pattern.

Bake for 25 minutes until golden

Number of Servings: 16

Net Carbs Per Serving: 1g

Coconut Cookies

Ingredients:

3 cups shredded unsweetened coconut flakes

1 cup coconut oil, melted

1/2 cup monk fruit sweetened maple syrup Can substitute for any liquid sweetener of choice

Directions:

Line a large plate or baking tray with parchment paper and set aside.

In a large mixing bowl, combine all your ingredients and mix very well. Lightly wet your hands then form small balls with the batter, placing them 1-2 inches apart on the lined baking tray.

Using a fork, press down onto each cookie. Refrigerate until firm.

Number of Servings: 20

Net Carbs Per Serving: 0g

Chocolate Fudge Cookie

Ingredients:

1/2 cup sweetener

1/2 cup cocoa powder

4 tablespoons butter

2 large egg

1 teaspoon vanilla

1 cup almond flour

1 teaspoon baking powder

1 pinch salt

Directions:

Combine cocoa powder and swerve confectioners sugar in a mixing bowl.

Add melted butter to mixture and combine with a hand mixer.

Once combined, add eggs, vanilla, and baking powder and mix again.

Now add the almond flour and mix one last time. You should have a fairly thick batter that can easily be shaped by hand.

Form into cookies and place on a greased baking sheet. The cookies will remain the shape you form them to after cooking. They do not expand too much.

Dust the tops of cookies with erythritol. (optional)

Bake at 350 for 12-15 minutes. Let cool and enjoy! These are great straight out of the freezer as well. These can be frozen for 2-3 months!

Number of Servings: 10

Net Carbs Per Serving: 2g

Coconut Cluster

Ingredients:

3.5 ounces of dark unsweetened baking chocolate

1 tablespoon of coconut oil

1/2 a tablespoon of confectioners erythritol sweetener

1 teaspoon of vanilla extract

1/2 a cup of sliced almonds

1/2 a cup of big coconut flakes or big chips

Directions:

Melt the baking chocolate and coconut oil together in a small sauce pan over low heat, whilst stirring.

When the chocolate is melted, add the sugar and vanilla and stir until mixed in.

Remove from the heat and mix in the almonds and coconut flakes.

Scoop the mixture into bite sized clusters and drop them onto parchment paper.

Let the clusters harden in the fridge for about 30 minutes.

Enjoy or store the clusters in an airtight container.

Number of Servings: 12

Net Carbs Per Serving: 2g

Almond Zucchini Cookies

Ingredients:

1/2 cup almond butter

1/2 cup packed zucchini, shredded (or 1/2 zucchini)

1 large egg

2 tablespoons coconut nectar (or other sweetener)

1/2 teaspoon baking soda

1/4 cup hemp seeds

1/2 teaspoon cinnamon

1/4 teaspoon ground nutmeg

1/2 teaspoon almond extract

Directions:

Pre-heat oven to 350f degrees and line a baking sheet.

Mix all ingredients together with a hand or stand mixer until your cookie batter comes together.

Scoop cookies out onto parchment paper

Bake for 10-12 minutes and let cool for a few minutes before serving. Store in a cookie jar to keep them soft and chewy

Number of Servings: 12

Chocolate Cloud Cookies

Ingredients:

8 large egg whites, room temperature

¼ teaspoon cream of tartar

½ teaspoon pure vanilla extract

6 tablespoons raw cacao powder

4 teaspoons shredded, dairy-free dark chocolate

¼ teaspoon sea salt

Directions:

Preheat the oven to 300°F. Prepare a baking sheet with parchment paper.

Use a hand mixer to beat egg whites, cream of tartar, salt and vanilla in a large mixing bowl for 5 minutes, until soft peaks form.

Carefully fold in raw cacao powder and shredded dark chocolate into the egg white mixture until just combined, being careful not to overmix.

Drop a large spoonful of the batter onto the prepared baking sheet to form two dozen cookies.

Bake 22-25 minutes, or until the cookies have hardened on the outside. They should feel dry, yet have a soft texture.

Transfer cookies to a wire baking rack to cool a few minutes before enjoying.

Number of Servings: 24

Chocolate Sea Salt Cookies

Ingredients:

3/4 cup coconut oil, room temperature

2 eggs

1 teaspoon vanilla extract

3/4 cup fruit sweetener

2 tablespoons unsweetened cocoa powder

1/2 teaspoon baking soda

1/2 teaspoon salt

1/4 teaspoon cream of tartar

2 cups almond flour

Flakey sea salt

Directions:

Preheat oven to 350 degrees and line two baking sheets with parchment paper.

In a medium-sized bowl, using a hand mixer, mix together coconut oil, eggs, and vanilla extract until well-combined.

To the same bowl, add monk fruit sweetener, cocoa powder, baking soda, salt, and cream of tartar. Mix using hand mixer until fully incorporated.

One cup at a time, add almond flour and mix together with hand mixer.

Form dough into balls and lightly press down and place on prepared baking sheet (NOTE: cookies will spread when baking so be sure to place them about 2-3 inches apart.)

Add desired amount of sea salt to top of each cookie.

One baking sheet at a time, bake cookies until toothpick can be poked into center and comes out cleanly, about 15-18 minutes.

Remove from oven and allow to cool completely.

Once cooled, carefully peel the parchment paper away from the bottom of the cookie.

Serve and enjoy!

Number of Servings: 15

Net Carbs Per Serving: 1.6g

Cinnamon Butter Cookie

Ingredients:

2 cups almond meal/flour

1/2 cup salted butter (softened at room temp)

1 egg

1 teaspoon vanilla extract

1 teaspoon ground cinnamon

1 teaspoon liquid stevia

Directions:

Preheat oven to 300

Add all ingredients to a mixing bowl and mix until well combined.

Roll into 15 balls and place on a greased cookie sheet.

Place in the oven and bake for 5 minutes.

Remove and press dough down with a fork.

Return to oven and cook for 18-20 minutes.

Allow to cool for 5 minutes.

Number of Servings: 24

Net Carbs Per Serving: 1g

Snickerdoodle Crème Cookies

Ingredients:

Cookie:

1 cup coconut flour

2 teaspoon cinnamon

1 teaspoon baking soda

3/4 teaspoon cream of tartar

1/2 teaspoon salt

1 cup Swerve

2 eggs

2 teaspoons vanilla extract

1/2 cup butter, softened

Outing Coating: Surkin Gold brown sugar sub, plus 1/2 tsp cinnamon

Filling:

1 cup Confectioners Swerve

1 teaspoon vanilla extract

1/2 cup butter, softened

2 tablespoons milk

Directions:

Preheat oven to 350 degrees.

In a stand mixer add the first 6 ingredients and mix on low to combine.

Add the eggs, vanilla and butter to the mixture and blend until incorporated. Using a 1 inch cookie scoop, roll into balls and place on a baking sheet lined with parchment or silpat.

Make 72 balls. Roll each in brown sugar sub or granulated Swere mixed with cinnamon.

Flatten balls slightly and bake for 12 minutes.

Cool completely.

Make filling by adding ingredients to a stand mixer and mix on high until smooth.

Spread on half the cookies and place another cookie over the filling to make 36 sandwich cookies.

Number of Servings: 36

Net Carbs Per Serving: 2g

Cream Cheese Brownie

Ingredients:

Cream Cheese Filling:

8 oz cream cheese softened

1 large egg

1 teaspoon vanilla

1/4 cup powdered erythritol –or– 12 drops liquid stevia

Brownies:

2 large eggs

1/4 cup powdered erythritol (or swerve)

6 tablespoons butter unsalted

2.5 oz unsweetened baker's chocolate

1 teaspoon vanilla

1/4 cup coconut flour

1/2 teaspoon salt

1/2 teaspoon baking powder

Directions:

Preheat oven to 350 and butter an 8x8 pan. Set aside.

In a medium bowl, beat cream cheese until whipped. Mix in egg, vanilla and powdered erythritol OR 12 drops liquid stevia until well combined. Set aside.

In a large bowl, beat eggs until they are frothy. Stir in powdered erythritol and let stand about 5 minutes.

In a small microwave safe bowl, melt butter and chocolate for 30 second intervals stirring between heatings, until chocolate is completely melted.

Add vanilla, salt, baking powder and melted chocolate to the bowl with the eggs and stir well.

Slowly stir in coconut flour (in 1 tbsp increments works best)

Once mixed, spread 3/4 of the brownie mixture into the prepared pan.

Spoon the cream cheese mixture on top and smooth it around.

Spread the rest of the brownie mixture on top of the cream cheese mixture to create a marbled look.

Bake 25-30 minutes or until a toothpick insterted in the center comes out clean

Number of Servings: 9

Net Carbs Per Serving: 2g

Cinnamon Roll Mug Cake

Ingredients:

2 tablespoons vanilla protein powder

1/2 teaspoon baking powder

1 tablespoon coconut flour

1/2 teaspoon cinnamon

1 T granulated sweetener of choice*

1 large egg –or- 1/4 cup liquid egg whites

1/4 cup milk of choice

1/4 teaspoon vanilla extract

1 teaspoon granulated sweetener of choice

1/2 teaspoon cinnamon

For the glaze:

1 tablespoons coconut butter, melted

1/2 teaspoon milk of choice

pinch cinnamon

Directions:

Grease an oven safe dish with cooking spray and add the protein powder, baking powder, coconut flour, cinnamon, sweetener of choice and mix well.

Add the egg/whites and mix into the dry mixture. Add the milk of choice and vanilla extract- If batter is too crumbly, continue adding milk of choice until a very thick batter is formed. granulated sweetener of choice and extra cinnamon and swirl over the top

Bake in the oven at 350 Farenheit for 8-15 minutes, depending on consistency desired- Mug cake is cooked once a toothpick comes out 'just' clean from the center.

Number of Servings: 1

Cocoa Butter Blondie

Ingredients:

6 tablespoons cacao butter

4 tablespoons butter unsalted

2 large eggs

1/2 cup erythritol

1 teaspoon vanilla extract

2 tablespoons coconut cream

1/4 cup almond flour

2 tablespoons coconut flour

1/4 teaspoon baking soda

1/4 teaspoon salt

1/2 oz. dark chocolate chopped

2 tablespoons walnuts or any nuts or chia optional

Directions:

Preheat the oven to 320°F (160°C) and line an 8" square baking pan with some parchment paper. Next, measure out all of the ingredients.

Put cacao butter and butter into a microwave-safe bowl. Let the two melt in a microwave for a minute and a half. Stir the butter until there are no lumps left. If needed, microwave for another minute or so. Set aside to cool.

Using a hand electric mixer, mix the eggs, erythritol, and vanilla extract. Add the coconut cream and mix again.

Pour in the cooled butter and mix until the mixture gets denser and creamy.

Sieve and mix the two flours, baking soda, and salt. Add this flour mixture to the cream and combine well with a rubber spatula. Add the chopped chocolate and stir well again.

Put the mixture into the prepared baking pan and spread it out evenly, using a spatula.

Put in the oven and bake for 30 minutes. When a toothpick is inserted in the center, it isn't necessary that it comes out completely clean. You want the blondies to remain somewhat fudgy in the middle. Don't over-bake.

When done baking, take the whole batch out of the pan, together with the parchment paper, and let it cool down. When cooled, cut into 20 more or less equal size blondies.

Number of Servings: 20

Net Carbs Per Serving: 0.6g

Pound Cake

Ingredients:

Pound Cake:

2 ½ cups almond flour

½ cup unsalted butter, softened

1 ½ cups erythritol

8 whole eggs, room temperature

1 ½ teaspoons vanilla extract

½ teaspoon lemon extract

½ teaspoon salt

8 ounces cream cheese

1 ½ teaspoons baking powder

Glaze:

¼ cup powdered erythritol

3 tablespoons heavy whipping cream

½ teaspoon vanilla extract

Directions:

Preheat oven to 350°F. Toss in room temperature butter, softened cream cheese, and erythritol into a mixing bowl.

Cream together the butter and erythritol until smooth. Then, add in softened chunks of cream cheese and blend together until smooth.

Add in the eggs, lemon extract, and vanilla extract in with the blended ingredients. Blend with a hand mixer until smooth.

In a medium sized bowl: mix together the almond flour, baking powder, and salt.

Slowly add in the ingredients from the medium sized bowl into the batter. Use a hand blender to blend the clumps until very smooth.

Pour batter into a loaf pan. Bake for 60 - 120 minutes at 350F or until smooth in the middle when tested with a toothpick.

If creating a glaze: blend together the powdered erythritol, vanilla extract, and heavy whipping cream until smooth. Wait until the pound cake is fully cooled from the oven before spreading the glaze on top.

Number of Servings: 16

Net Carbs Per Serving: 2.49

Lemon Coconut Cake

Ingredients:

Coconut Cake:

1/2 cup coconut flour

5 eggs

1/4 cup natvia (or erythritol)

1/2 cup butter melted

1/2 lemon juiced

1/2 teaspoon lemon zest

1/2 teaspoon xanthan gum

1/2 teaspoon salt

Icing:

1 cup cream cheese

3 tablespoons Natvia Or Swerve

1 teaspoon vanilla extract

½ tsp lemon zest

Directions:

Separate the egg whites and yolks. Beat the egg whites until they form white peaks.

Into the same bowl, place the rest of the cake ingredients (including the egg yolks) into the bowl. Mix until well combined.

Pour into a greased loaf tin (9" X 5")

Bake at 180 C (355 F) for 45 mins (fan forced)

Whilst the cake is in the oven, beat the cream cheese, Nativa, vanilla extract and lemon zest together with an electric beater.

Set aside and ice the cake once it has finished cooking.

Slice and enjoy

Number of Servings: 10

Net Carbs Per Serving: 1g

Brownie Cupcakes

Ingredients:

1/2 cup almond flour

1/4 cup unsweetened cocoa powder

1 teaspoon baking powder

1/4 teaspoon salt

4 ounces unsweetened chocolate chopped

1/2 cup granular erythritol

1 1/2 teaspoons vanilla extract divided

1/4 teaspoon liquid stevia extract

5 large eggs

1/2 (8-ounce) package cream cheese softened

1/2 cup powdered erythritol

3/4 cup unsalted butter

3 tablespoons unsalted butter softened

Directions:

Preheat the oven to 325°F and line a muffin pan with paper liners.

Whisk together the almond flour, cocoa powder, baking powder, and salt in a bowl.

In a small saucepan, whisk together ¾ cup butter and the unsweetened chocolate.

When the chocolate and butter are melted, stir smooth then whisk in the granular erythritol, 1 teaspoon vanilla extract, and the liquid stevia extract.

Remove from heat and let cool for 5 minutes.

Once cooled, whisk in the eggs, one at a time, then stir in the dry ingredients until smooth.

Spoon the batter into the prepared pan, filling them about 2/3 full.

Bake the cupcakes for 16 to 20 minutes until a knife inserted in the center comes out clean then cool to room temperature.

To prepare the frosting, beat the cream cheese and the remaining butter until creamy.

Beat the powdered erythritol and ½ teaspoon vanilla extract until light and fluffy then frost the cupcakes as desired.

Number of Servings: 12

Net Carbs Per Serving: 2.5g

Cinnamon Bundt Cake

Ingredients:

2 cups almond flour

1-2 tablespoon coconut flour

2 teaspoons alminum-free baking powder

2 tablespoons cinnamon

2 tablespoons Stevia powder

5 large eggs

3 tablespoons melted coconut oil (or butter)

3 tablespoons water

Cream Cheese Frosting:

4 oz cream cheese

2 tablespoons melted coconut oil (or butter)

4 tablespoons heavy cream

1 tablespoon Stevia powder

1 teaspoon vanilla extract

2-3 tablespoons chopped nuts (Optional)

Directions:

Cake:

Preheat the oven to 170 C / 325 F.

In a large bowl, combine all the dry ingredients and mix well.

In a separate bowl, mix well all the wet ingredients until whitish.

Add the egg mixture to the dry mixture and stir with a spatula.

Pour the batter into a (greased) 10 inch bundt pan.

Bake for 30 - 40 minutes.

Let cool on a wire rack.

Cream Cheese Frosting:

Cream together the cream cheese, coconut oil, heavy cream and stevia.

Transfer the mixture to a saucepan and heat it over low heat for 20 - 30 seconds. Remove from heat.

Add the vanilla to the saucepan and mix well.

Pour the frosting over the cooled cinnamon cake.

Sprinkle the chopped nuts.

Chill until the frosting is set or serve immediately.

Number of Servings: 10

Net Carbs Per Serving: 6.2g

Carrot Cake

Ingredients:

3/4 cup erythritol

3/4 cup butter

1 tablespoon Blackstrap molasses (optional)

1 teaspoon vanilla extract

1/2 teaspoon pineapple extract (optional)

4 large egg

2 1/2 cup almond flour

2 teaspoons gluten-free baking powder

2 teaspoon cinnamon

1/2 teaspoon sea salt

2 1/2 cup carrots (grated, measured loosely packed after grating)

1 1/2 cup pecans (chopped; divided into 1 cup and 1/2 cup)

2 full recipes Sugar-free cream cheese frosting

Directions:

Preheat the oven to 350 degrees F. Line two 9-inch round cake pans with parchment paper. (Use springform pans if you have them.) Grease the bottom and sides.

In a large bowl, cream together the butter and erythritol, until fluffy. Beat in the molasses (if using), vanilla extract, and pineapple extract (if using). Beat in the eggs, one at a time. Set aside.

In another bowl, mix together the almond flour, baking powder, cinnamon, and sea salt. Stir the dry ingredients into the bowl with the wet ingredients.

Stir in the grated carrots. Fold 1 cup of the chopped pecans, reserving the remaining 1/2 cup.

Transfer the batter evenly among the two prepared baking pans. Bake for 30-35 minutes, until the top is spring-y.

Let the cakes cool in the pans for 10 minutes, then transfer to a wire rack to cool completely.

Meanwhile, make the sugar-free frosting according to the instructions here. (Double the recipe by entering "12" into the box for # of servings on that page.)

When the cake has cooled to room temperature, place the bottom layer on a plate or cake stand. Frost, then add the top layer and frost again. Top with the remaining chopped pecans.

Number of Servings: 16

Net Carbs Per Serving: 5.5g

Butter Cake

Ingredients:

Cake:

2 1/2 cups almond flour

1/4 cup coconut flour

1/4 cup unflavoured whey protein powder

1 tablespoon baking powder

1/2 teaspoon salt

1 cup butter softened

1 cup Swerve Granular

5 large eggs room temperature.

2 teaspoons vanilla extract

1/2 cup whipping cream

1/2 cup water

Butter Glaze:

5 tablespoons butter

1/3 cup Swerve granular

2 tablespoons water

1 teaspoon vanilla extract

Garnish:

1-2 tablespoons Confectioner's Swerve

Directions:

Preheat oven to 325F. Grease a bundt cake pan very well and then dust with a few tbsp of almond flour.

In a medium bowl, whisk together the almond flour, coconut flour, whey protein, baking powder, and salt.

In a large bowl, beat the butter and the sweetener together until light and creamy. Beat in the eggs and vanilla extract. Beat in the almond flour mixture and then beat in the whipping cream and water until well combined.

Transfer the batter to the prepared baking pan and smooth the top. Bake 50 to 60 minutes, until golden brown and the cake is firm to the touch. A tester inserted in the center should come out clean.

Butter Glaze: In a small saucepan over low heat, melt the butter and sweetener together. Whisk until well combined. Whisk in the water and vanilla extract.

While the cake is still warm and in the pan, poke holes all over with a skewer. Pour the glaze over and let cool completely in the pan.

Gently loosen the sides with a knife or thin rubber spatula, then flip out onto a serving platter. Dust with powdered sweetener.

Serve with lightly sweetened whipped cream and fresh berries.

Number of Servings: 16

Net Carbs Per Serving: 3g

Avocado Brownies

Ingredients:

2 large eggs

1 medium, ripe, hass avocado (3/4 cup)

1/4 cup melted ghee (lard or coconut oil)

3-4 tablespoons unsweetened, unsalted almond butter (or sunflower seed butter for nut-free)

1/2 teaspoon baking soda

1/4 teaspoon salt

1/3 cup Swerve (erythritol) or preferred granulated sweetener

1/3 cup cacao powder

1/2 teaspoon vanilla extract

Directions:

Pre-heat oven to 350F.

Line a small baking dish with parchment paper.

In the bowl of your blender or food processor combine all of the ingredients.

Blend om medium, low power until just smooth. No more than 40 seconds.

Use a spatula to transfer the batter to the baking dish and smooth it out evenly.

Top with fun things if you wish

Bake for 25-30 minutes. If you're using a metal baking dish it could be less time. Check it after 20 minutes. It's done when the top begins to crack and it has turned a deep brown color. Use a toothpick to check the center, if it comes out crumbly, but not streaked you're good.

Remove from the oven and let it cool for 15 minutes before handling.

Pick it up, carefully, by the parchment paper and set it on a cutting board.

Cut into 8 squares! Enjoy!

Number of Servings: 10

Net Carbs Per Serving: 8g

Chocolate Tart

Ingredients:

1 1/4 cup almond flour

3/4 cup unsweetened shredded coconut

1 medium egg

3/4 cup coconut cream

1/4 cup coconut oil melted

10 drops stevia or more, depending on your sweet tooth

2 tablespoons and 1 teaspoon cacao powder unsweetened

1 teaspoon vanilla essence

pinch of salt

small handful of chopped hazelnuts to garnish

Directions:

Preheat the oven to 350 F.

Mix the shredded coconut, almond flour and the egg with a stick blender or in a food processor until it forms a doughy ball.

Press the dough into a loaf tin lined with baking paper.

Bake the tart base for ca 20 minutes or until lightly browned. Remove from the oven and let cool.

Now make the chocolate ganache. Melt the coconut oil, then stir in the coconut cream, cacao powder, vanilla essence, pinch of salt and the stevia or powdered erythritol. Taste and adjust the sweetener if necessary.

Pour into the cooled tart base and place in the fridge until fully set (ca 1 1/2 hours).

Before serving, dry-roast some chopped hazelnuts in a pan on medium heat until golden. Sprinkle over the tart and enjoy.

Number of Servings: 8

Net Carbs Per Serving: 1.5g